DATE DUE

Fish for The Grand Lady

COLIN BOOTMAN

Holiday House / New York

Copyright © 2006 by Colin Bootman
All Rights Reserved
Printed in the United States of America
The artwork was created with oil paint on canvas.
The text typeface is Fritz.
www.holidayhouse.com
First Edition
1 3 5 7 9 10 8 6 4 2

Library of Congress Cataloging-in-Publication Data
Bootman, Colin.
Fish for the Grand Lady / by Colin Bootman.— 1st ed.
p. cm.
Summary: In Trinidad, two brothers try fishing in a new place,
hoping to bring home a big catch for their grandmother.
ISBN 0-8234-1898-7
[1. Fishing—Fiction. 2. Brothers—Fiction. 3. Grandmothers—Fiction.
4. Trinidad and Tobago—Fiction.] I. Title.
PZ7.B64735Fi 2006
[E]—dc22
2004054166
ISBN-13: 978-0-8234-1898-5
ISBN-10: 0-8234-1898-7

For my Grand Lady, Irene Charles,
and my big brother, Derrick Forde

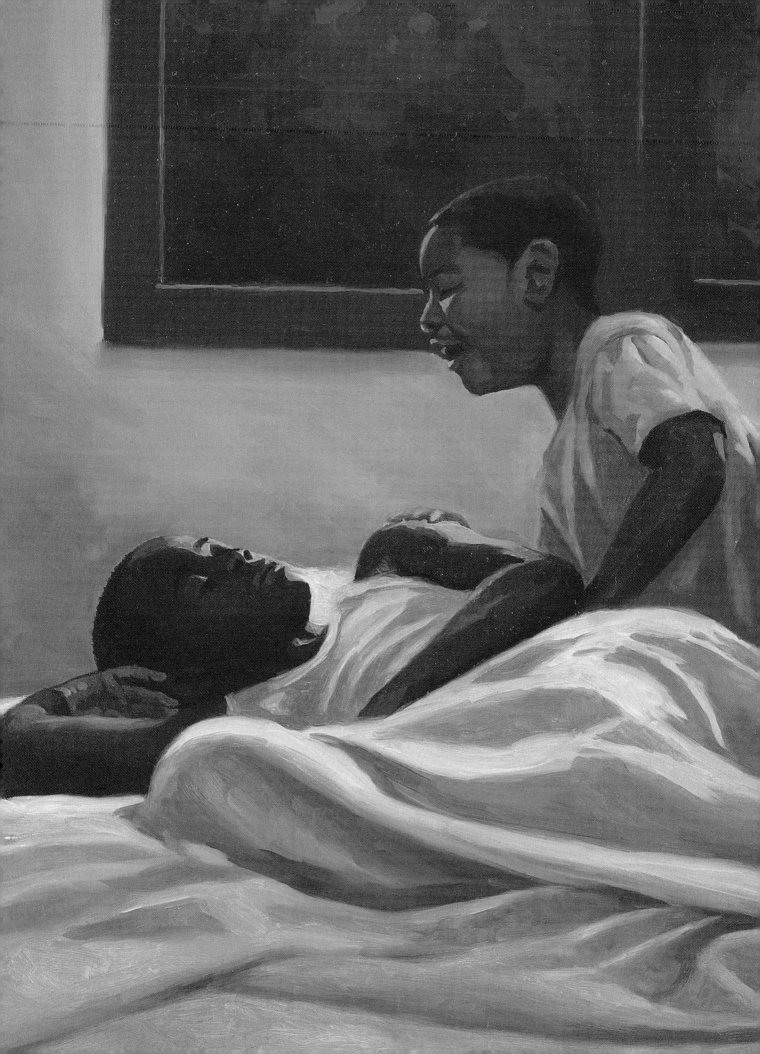

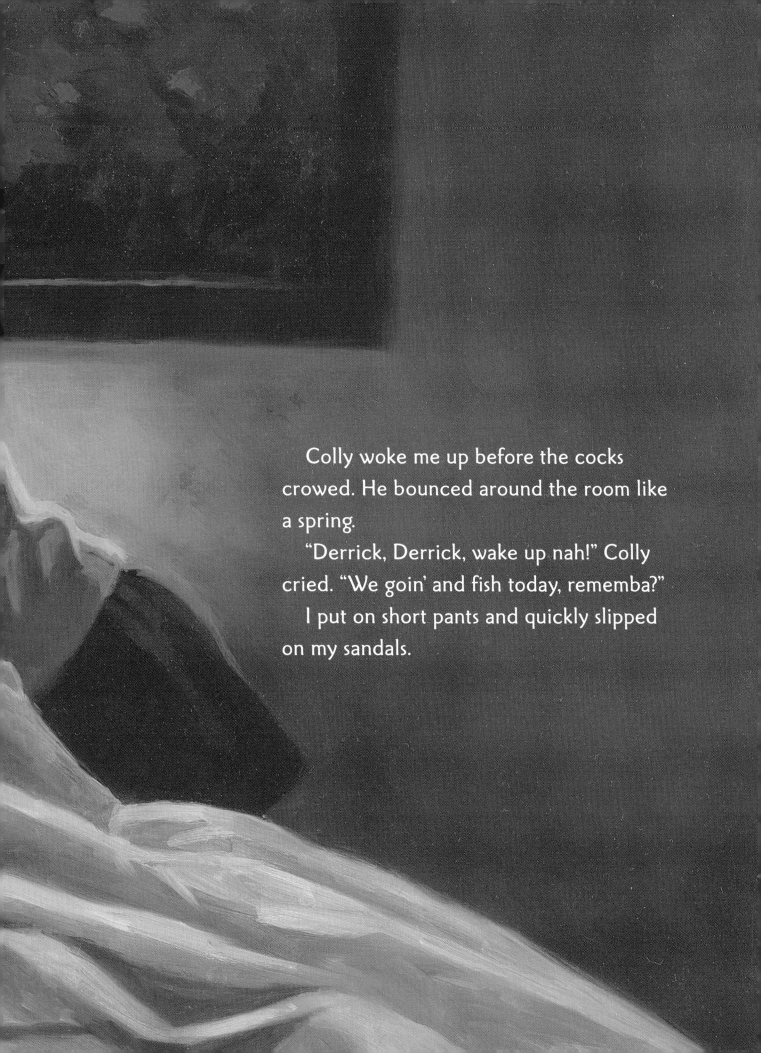

Colly woke me up before the cocks crowed. He bounced around the room like a spring.

"Derrick, Derrick, wake up nah!" Colly cried. "We goin' and fish today, rememba?"

I put on short pants and quickly slipped on my sandals.

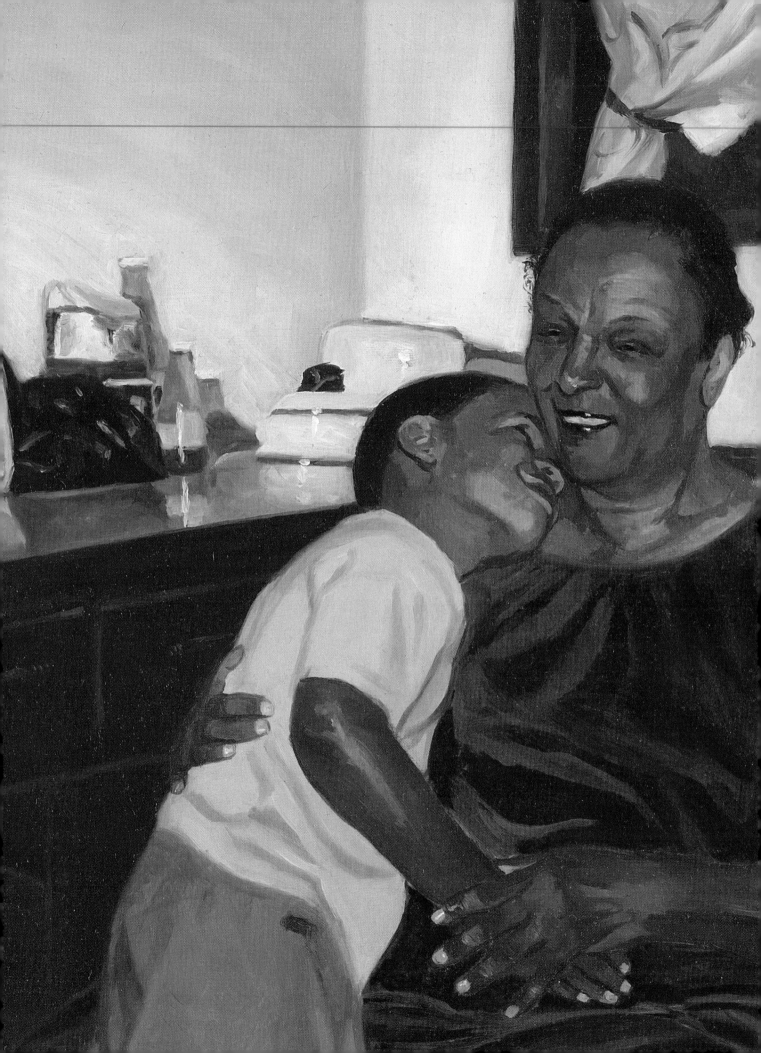

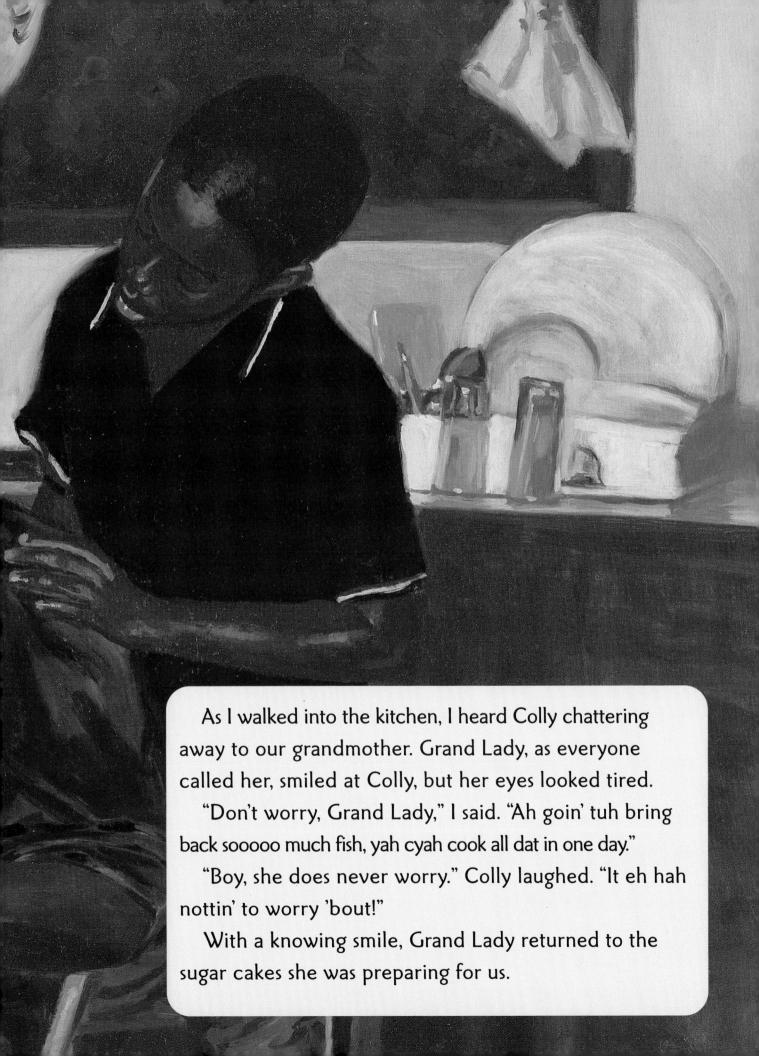

As I walked into the kitchen, I heard Colly chattering away to our grandmother. Grand Lady, as everyone called her, smiled at Colly, but her eyes looked tired.

"Don't worry, Grand Lady," I said. "Ah goin' tuh bring back sooooo much fish, yah cyah cook all dat in one day."

"Boy, she does never worry." Colly laughed. "It eh hah nottin' to worry 'bout!"

With a knowing smile, Grand Lady returned to the sugar cakes she was preparing for us.

"Come orn nah, Colly," I said. "We hah to get hooks from Wong an dem fuh we to go fishin'." I took the sugar cakes from Grand Lady, and Colly shot out the door right behind me.

"Be very careful crossin' the main road, yuh hear me?" Grand Lady called after us.

"Buh, Derrick, how come we passin' here? Ent de main road does take we up by St. Joseph River? Ent Gampert Stream closer? Dah is not wey we does always go fishin'?" Colly asked.

"Stee . . . eups! Doh ask meh so much ah questions nah, boy! Shucks, man! Wey we goin' is ah secret, bwo . . . o . . . oy," I answered. "Grand Lady tell me 'bout it. Boy, we could ketch more fish day dan in all ah Gampert Stream, oui."

"More fish dan we could eat in a day?" Colly asked.

"Plenty more fish, fish like peas!" I answered.

The purple-blue sky started to lighten. Warm shades of orange and red peeped over the hilltops. I held Colly's hand as we crossed the main road. On the other side, coconut trees loomed high over tin roofs, dancing with the breeze.

The scent of mangoes, soursops, bananas, star apples, and sapodillas sweetened the air. The crowing cocks and the crunch of the gravel beneath our feet were the only sounds we heard along the roadside.

It was still early when we arrived at Curepe Junction, but people already crowded the market. Heads snapped and popped as bodies danced to and fro, in and around the wooden stands.

Some people smiled, some laughed, some shouted, and many just talked quietly. The fish man sang, "Freeesh fish, freeesh fish. Redfish, kingfish, carite. Come an get yuh fresh fish."

Mr. Wong smiled when we reached his stand. He asked, "What you want for this morning?"

Before I could answer, Mrs. Wong brought the hooks and placed them before us. She stared at me for a long time.

"Why your face so serious?" she asked. "Life can be hard, I know, but always remember to smile. Smiling face is smiling heart."

"Ah smiling, Mrs. Wong!" Colly exclaimed.

"Well, Derrick should too." Mrs. Wong nodded.

We thanked them and left the stand.

The trail up St. Joseph's Mountain was narrow, just big enough for two people. Insects and lizards scuttled along the trail. Birds settled high above us as we shuffled through the forest.

Colly looked up at me. "Yah tellin' meh de truth 'bout dis place? Eh?"

I smiled and said, "It right day over de hill. Listen, Colly! Listen! Yah cyah hear de river?"

The river snaked itself around the mountain. Colly
ran down the hill, stopping just above the water's edge.
Once we found enough worms, we crept down the
river's muddy bank, sat on a large blue stone where the
water was calm, cast our lines in, and waited. Several
times we got a nibble and each time we found that the
worms disappeared.

By noon our snacks were gone. "It still early, boy. Dem fish go start tuh bite jus now," Colly said.

I shook my head. "Maybe Grand Lady was wrong, oui." I said. "Maybe dis place ent secret at all!"

Colly's eyes filled with tears. "Buh Grand Lady never wrong, Derrick."

I threw the bucket of worms into the water. "I vex oui, boy! Leh we go home, yes! Hmmm!" I grumbled, and stormed back up the bank.

Then a little hand touched my arm. "Derrick, Derrick," Colly whispered excitedly. "Look! Look! Look at de bucket."

"Shhh, doh move, Colly. Doh move," I whispered, and climbed back down the bank. I tiptoed into the water. In one single motion I snatched the handle and swooped the bucket out of the water.

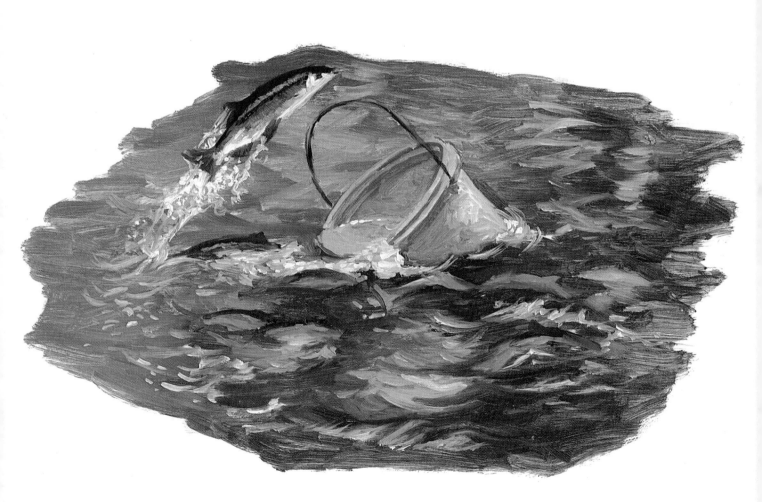

Just then Colly lost his balance and tumbled down the muddy bank into the river. Now we were both wet and laughing. But in my hand was the dripping bucket filled with splashing fish.

On the walk home
we took turns carrying
our catch.

Grand Lady was in
the kitchen, stirring a
pot filled with vegetables.
I held up the bucket of
fish for her to see.

"Look, Grand Lady.
Derrick ketch more
fish dan we could
eat in a whole day!"
Colly said.

"Much, much more," Grand Lady said, and smiled.

Author's Note

Although English is the official language of Trinidad, the island's dialect reflects the many different peoples who have settled there. The Amerindians, indigenous people who were living on the island before the time of Christopher Columbus, themselves represented several languages. The Spanish were joined by fellow Catholics from France and Haiti, who immigrated to the island early on, bringing their own tongue. Enslaved blacks from Africa imported their own languages. Later, under British rule, immigrants from India and China became part of the cultural makeup of Trinidad. Within its colorful English, traces of Spanish, French, Chinese, West African, South Asian, and Amerindian languages flavor the everyday vocabulary.

In this story the reader will come across words and phrases that are common in the Trinidadian dialect. The following are some of these words and phrases:

Ah = I or a

buh = but

cyah = cannot

dah = that

dan = than

day = there or they

de = the

dem = them

dis = this

doh = do not

ent = isn't

fuh = for

tuh = to

yah = you

yuh = your

come orn nah = let's go

I vex oui, boy! = I am very angry

Leh we go = Let us go

"Stee . . . eups!" = a sound made by sucking air through one's teeth

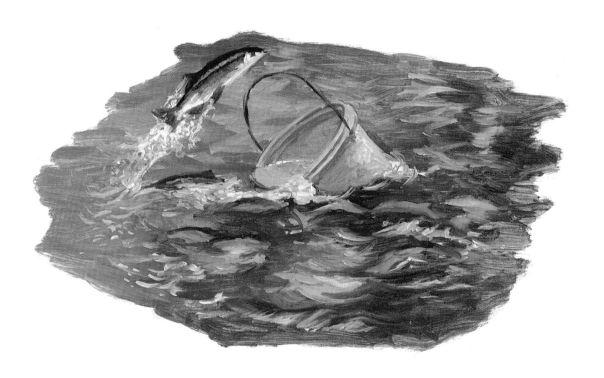